SMILE BETTER YOUR DAY

Make a Happy Start To Your Day. Smile As You Begin Your Day.

James D. Miller

Disclaimer

This eBook has been written for information purposes only. Every effort has been made to make this eBook as complete and accurate as possible.

However, there may be mistakes in typography or content. Also, this eBook provides information only up to the publishing date. Therefore, this eBook should be used as a guide - not as the ultimate source.
The purpose of this eBook is to educate. The author and the publisher do not warrant that the information contained in this eBook is fully complete and shall not be responsible for any errors or omissions.

The author and publisher shall have neither liability nor responsibility to any person or entity with respect to any loss or damage caused or alleged to be caused directly or indirectly by this eBook.

Table of Content

Introduction

Sometimes, whether it's a trip, a graduation, or a wedding, we make big plans that we think will make our lives happier.

However, we can rely on the straightforward joys in life to provide us with lasting happiness. The thankfulness we experience will spread to other areas as well as we recognize and enjoy the little things. Here are a few easy joys that are worthwhile trying to enjoy often.

Just-cut grass

In every sense, enjoying freshly cut grass is delightful. Its fresh scent and texture are energizing to the senses as you walk on it barefoot. As long as the weather permits it, try to do this at least a few times a year.

Smiles Transmitted and Received

What better method to enjoy a basic pleasure without spending any money? Be sure to smile at strangers you pass on the street in addition to your friends.
You'll be astounded at how satisfying it is to see other people's astonishment, followed by their grins in response.

The Endorphin Rush after Exercise

You will get an endorphin surge as a reward for working out vigorously. These organic, uplifting substances will undoubtedly make your day better. Exercise first thing in the morning to benefit from the endorphin high and be more effective the rest of the day.

Eating Your Favorite Cuisine

Permit yourself to sometimes indulge in your favorite meal, even if it's not very nutritious. You'll receive a little increase of pleasure from the sensation of your favorite cuisine. Use this strategy to make your favorite meal taste even better than normal since studies have shown that if you skip eating anything for some time, the next time you do, it will be even more delightful.

Piping-hot Coffee or Tea

Some of us get by each day on our coffee or tea. Even when it becomes routine, it may be quite enjoyable. Take some quiet time to savor each sip of your preferred beverage.

Constructing Snow Angels

This isn't only for children. Don some warm clothing, and just dive into the snow. Making snow angels may be a lot of pure fun, so don't let your stupid feelings about it mar the experience.

Up till It Hurts to Laugh

Laughter is therapeutic. At least once a day, everyone should have the chance to laugh themselves silly. Take some time to laugh your tension away, whether you do it with a buddy who can write humor or by watching a fantastic movie.

Receiving a Massage

Try getting a massage if you've never had one. Your worries will seem to be melting away during this hour of complete relaxation. Even massages are available to many people as part of work perks.

Rainy Day Walking

One of the great, basic joys of life is strolling in the rain. Go outdoors with warm clothing and with or without an umbrella. While strolling, let the rain splatter over your face, and be sure to jump in at least one puddle just for nostalgia's sake.

The most expensive entertainment might be difficult to locate. Spend some time enjoying one of these straightforward joys rather than holding off until your next getaway. Every day will be filled with immense pleasure if you can learn to appreciate the little things that are right in front of you.

Chapter 1: Happiness

The concept of real happiness differs from person to person. "While a person's happiness frequently relies on their safety and well-being—on their salary—it also depends on their beliefs," said certified mental health therapist Billy Roberts.

Of course, individuals are led by various ideals. For some, worth rests in power; others find value in security or self-care. "A person who is motivated by power can have different financial demands than someone who is driven by security," Roberts stated. These variables may impact a person's happiness or sense of happiness, influencing the amount of money they genuinely need to be content emotionally.

"At the end of the day, the wage should support a value-driven lifestyle," Roberts added, "so the number is less essential than that figure enabling a person to drive in their 'values lane,' so to speak."

Does Happiness Increase With Income?

This article from 2021 in Proceedings of the National Academy of Sciences (PNAS) looks into the convoluted and complex link between money and well-being. The findings revealed that happiness increased the higher a person's income grows. Meaning that the more money we earn, the happier we become (or rather, we have the resources to acquire the goods or experiences that in turn make us happy) (or rather, we have the means to buy the things or experiences that in turn make us happy).

Does Poverty Affect Happiness?

On the other hand, folks with little income may be suffering greater stress. Licensed clinical psychologist and psychology professor Margaret Sala, Ph.D., who practices in Connecticut, remarked that poverty might magnify the sense of misfortunes and pressures. In other words, those with lower income levels may enhance feelings of sadness or other unpleasant emotions.

Illness may also be a factor that impacts happiness. "Illness may be significantly worse for individuals who are impoverished and unable to seek medical treatment," Dr. Sala remarked. Another example from Dr. Sala: not obtaining assistance with onerous tasks—such as childcare or home cleaning—that others with more affluent lives frequently don't need to worry about.

Does Stress Affect Happiness?

But, Dr. Sala claimed that some persons with greater earnings may not be able to appreciate minor joys in life owing to hectic and time-demanding work. A poll in 2018 from LinkedIn indicated that US workers earning more money reported considerably greater levels of stress—up to 68% more for top earners bringing in over $200,000. While these larger salaries purchase joys such as wonderful trips and dinners at restaurants, Dr. Sala stated that stress might play a crucial part in one's overall happiness.

What's the Science Behind It?

The relationship between money and happiness isn't simply an emotion or perception: There's a science behind the phenomena. "From a neuroscience standpoint, scarcity of money and resources signals to our brain that there is a danger to our life," said Renetta Weaver, doctor of metaphysics and certified clinical social worker. In reality, poverty may affect a person's cognitive function, changing the way they think and diminishing performance in verbal memory and processing speed, according to this study from Science.

Can You Be Happy Without Money?

In the case that money can't genuinely purchase happiness, how can individuals be content with what they have, regardless of income level? "If we don't associate money and goods to our worth and value, we find satisfaction in the things that money can't buy," Weaver said, "such as quality time and experiences with oneself and others."

Milana Perepyolkina, an international bestseller author of two books on happiness, warned that people mistake pleasure with happiness, suggesting correlations between pay and emotional well-being may not be realistic. "If you eat a piece of cake, you get joy," Perepyolkina remarked. "As soon as you are done, the joy is gone. When you spend money, you enjoy pleasure. Several hours later, this joy is likewise gone."

Perepyolkina added that even those individuals "who live in extremely low circumstances, such as temporary plastic tents with all of their things fitting in one bag, you will see pleasant, brilliant grins," Perepyolkina stated. "How can someone who has absolutely nothing be so happy? This is because they are appreciative for what they have: their life, their family, and their community."

Money Can Buy You a Limited Amount of Happiness

Studies have proven that yes, having enough money to fulfill your needs and those of your family does create pleasure. People living in poverty are often less joyful than those whose needs are supplied. Being able to pay for your expenses and having enough to get by financially can help you succeed in feeling joyful.

Money Brings Stresses of Its Own

There is a tension that goes along with having money. Whether you have a little or a lot, you undoubtedly know about this tension. There is the stress of knowing you need to spend what you have carefully, as well as the reality that individuals with ulterior purposes are attracted to those who are monetarily fortunate.

Not About What Comes in But What Goes Out

It is not so much the quantity of money that you earn that secures your pleasure, but rather what you are spending it on and where it is going on the way out. There are several strategies for using money that might enable you to feel more fulfilled. Where you place your money and who gets it may make a difference as to whether you gained anything by having had it.

Spend on Experiences, Not Things

Buying more items is not proven to make a person happy. Although investing in products that will endure seems like a sensible choice, research reveals that we tend to adapt to what we receive. Having these items doesn't continue giving infinite delight.

We are more likely to enjoy long-term happiness when money is spent on activities that will offer us lasting memories. Whether this means going on vacation by yourself or with your family, or finding time to do something enjoyable now and then... make careful to build experiences rather than acquiring something that will just go away with time.

Give It Away

Giving is one of the most fulfilling things you can do with your money. Whether it is to charity or a buddy in need, find a way to give back and share what you have. This is a method to spend that will generate long-term personal gains.

The quick answer is no; you do not need money to be happy. Money may be beneficial, though, to minimize the stress that can lessen the enjoyment that you do have. No matter what amount of money you have, apply these strategies to help attain the degree of happiness you seek, and live a life full of delight.

Chapter 2: Don't sweat the minor things

We have all heard that we shouldn't sweat the minor things. Letting oneself become worried about the small things in life is one of the largest ways to bring unneeded pain into life's path.

We may prevent a lot of bad emotions, and even health concerns, just by learning not to allow the small things to get to us.

Focus on the Big Picture

When something tiny occurs that makes you want to anger, compare the moment's importance to everything else going on in your own life, and in the world around you. You may have spilled your cake mix on the floor an hour before your guests are set to arrive. Are your friends still going to appreciate you and enjoy the evening even if you don't have a freshly made cake for them? If so, maybe you should concentrate your energy elsewhere rather than berating yourself for this tiny error.

Remember That We All Make Mistakes

When anything tiny tries to shatter your mood and optimistic perspective, think about the reality that everyone makes errors. Whether it is yourself or someone else who triggered the circumstance that seems like a train crash, bear in mind that errors are a regular part of life that happens to everyone. Don't allow one unpleasant incident to catch you by surprise.

Forgive Others

It might be hard to forgive someone else when it seems like they have brought you more work and worry. When someone rear-ends your car, you may be inclined to strike out at them verbally. However, pause and think about how it may feel to be in their position. Don’t behave and feel as if you have never made a mistake, but choose empathy.

Forgive Yourself

Forgiving others may be an easy affair compared to forgiving yourself. There are often occasions when we treat ourselves worse than we would ever allow a friend to treat us.

When you are having a tough time forgiving yourself, think about how you would manage a comparable mistake committed by a dear friend. Stop and think before bullying yourself, and consider getting professional treatment if you can't\stop a cascade of negative thoughts every time you fall short of perfection.

Ask Yourself If It Will Matter in Ten Years

We all have issues, and often at the moment, any difficulty appears large. Perception is not necessarily the reality, however, and it is up to us to put our circumstances into perspective so that we may appropriately cope with whatever comes our way.

When anything unpleasant occurs in your life, ask yourself whether it will matter in 10 years. If it won't, let it go. If someone throws you the middle finger in traffic, you may be tempted to lose your cool, but it is just not worth it. Save your emotions for things that are life-altering and merit your complete focus.

When anything goes wrong, you have two alternatives. You may sink into a fury, or let it go. Making the decision not to sweat the minor things will bring your life-changing enjoyment, and you will be glad for your adjustment in perspective.

Chapter 3: How Happy are You?

A desire to be happy is something that practically everyone shares in common. But it is not always simple to produce happiness, nor to judge if you are happy once you believe you should be in this certain frame of mind.

Every life will have ups and downs, and thus it is good if we have a measure by which to assess whether we have attained happiness or not.

Do I Wake Up Excited about the Day?

This is a tell-tale clue of your inner contentment. Do you wake up each morning eager to face the day, or do you feel worried and fearful? It is tough to be joyful if you are starting each morning in a bad manner.

Do I Look Forward to My Main Occupation?

Whether you are working, attending school, or doing anything else... you should experience a feeling of eagerness when you think about being there. There are some things we must do, like pay the rent, therefore your choice to work may not be an option. You do, however, have a choice as to where you work. If you don't like it, modify it.

Do I Enjoy the People I Spend Most of My Time With?

The individuals you spend the most of your time with are the ones who will have the biggest effect on you. If they are harsh, negative and lack drive, chances are that you ultimately will become the same sort of person. If your buddies are not encouraging, find new ones. Spend your spare time with individuals who will cause your life to be more enjoyable, and will help you make wonderful memories that will offer long-term enjoyment.

Do I Like Who I Am?

A vital component of happiness is enjoying and appreciating yourself for who you are. If you don't, then you need to find out why. Make the required improvements, and then choose to accept yourself despite your shortcomings.

Do I Dread or Look Forward to My Future?

Happiness entails feeling confident and secure about your future. We live in unpredictable times, but it doesn't imply that we have to spend every day in terror. Grow your confidence in tiny ways, and seek therapy if you experience more than occasional tension when you think about the future ahead.

Do I Know My Life Purpose?

Everyone has a life purpose. There is something about you that makes you a unique gift to the world. If you have not learned this about yourself yet, your self-esteem will suffer, as will your pleasure. There are several quizzes and publications devoted to determining your life purpose. Consider spending your time studying more and uncovering what makes you feel most satisfied in life.

Being joyful is not a frivolous ambition. It is crucial to know how you are wired and what it takes to be satisfied with yourself and your life. By asking yourself these questions and then taking a minute to think about your answers, you will be well on your way to a life of real happiness.

Chapter 4: The Relationship Between Food And Happiness

If you compare the human body to a vehicle, food is exactly like petroleum which is burnt to provide energy. Without fuel, the automobile will not move. Likewise, without nourishment, the human body would lack the energy to work effectively. In reality, various studies have proved that hunger may drive someone to be furious.

When it comes to happiness and every other aspect of your life, food can hurt or cure. By learning about what meals to pick and avoid, you will be able to improve your body and mind, and embrace happiness.

Nutritious Meals That May Boost Your Mood

If you ask many individuals the reason why they eat, their reaction will usually be “to live” - but in truth, it extends beyond that. Have you noticed that you become delighted when you are presented with your favorite dish? The mere sight of some meals may induce the production of ‘feel-good chemicals in the brain like serotonin.

While there are scientific studies that show there is a link between food and mood especially happiness, the specifics of how this is done remain unknown partially because some of the results have been contradicting. For example, there is a scientific debate on which is the healthiest food. Some research reported the Mediterranean while others are in support of Paleo.

Expert Opinion On Food And Happiness

Irrespective of the study inconsistencies, if there is one thing that experts agree upon, it is that the food we consume has a big influence on our mood and emotions. In an interview, an expert and author of multiple books including Food & Mood, Elizabeth Somer stated, "There has been a growing body of research, both animal studies, and human studies, to indicate that we truly are what we eat, physiologically and mentally."

This makes a lot of sense given that the only location the brain which is in control of all emotions and mood receives its fuel completely from our food. Since it is difficult to explain the relationship, the influence is not fully ruled out.

Somer adds that the human brain has been programmed to survive and to seek pleasure and nutrients like fat, salt, and sugar are effective pleasure deliverers. The sight, smell, or recollection of these food categories is enough to drive the mouth wet.

This is because they promote the release of dopamine and serotonin which makes us feel happy.

Where Do Dopamine And Serotonin Come From?

A low amount of serotonin has been connected with depression. Well-known anti-depressants act by boosting the amount of serotonin. The primary amino acid needed for the production of serotonin is tryptophan. If there is no tryptophan in the body, serotonin cannot be created.

Tryptophan is contained in diets high in protein. Protein is created by the coming together of various amino acids and tryptophan happens to be one of the amino acids. Logically, one may wish to imagine that ingesting a protein-rich diet would prolong their pleasure because of the high quantity of tryptophan. Unfortunately, it is not true.

When protein is digested, over twenty amino acids are produced and they compete to reach the brain. Tryptophan loses out in the process. According to Somer, only an all-carb snack may raise the amounts of tryptophan which is subsequently employed as a precursor for serotonin. In the end, the objective should be to eat sensibly and remain healthy rather than seek a fast cure.

Foods to Boost Happiness

So you want to utilize what Mother Nature has to offer to increase your mood? Start by searching for foods that are rich in healthy fats. Our brains depend on certain fats, such as omega-3 fatty acids, and they do wonders for mood and enhancing happiness by enabling nerve cells to connect more effectively.

Walnuts, pumpkin seeds, and fish oil are fantastic methods to ingest them. Omega-3 fatty acids have been proven to be equally beneficial as typical antidepressant medicines for depression.

Berries are another fantastic method to improve your happiness. They include anthocyanins, which are useful to your brain since they maintain their function. Oranges, fresh peppers, and kiwi are strong in Vitamin C which combat stress. Leafy greens raise your folic acid intake, and even dark chocolate is proven to be a favorable mood booster. Bananas and dates are readily obtainable foods that are proven to impact serotonin levels favorably.

Your emotions and brain performance are also substantially influenced by dehydration, so be sure to keep well-hydrated by ingesting enough water.

Foods That Steal Your Joy

Sugar is the number one food to avoid if you desire to be happy. Sugar sets you up for a brief, deceptive rush of energy when you experience the sugar high, which is subsequently followed by a collapse. Sugar may also weaken your immune system and promote sadness.

Coffee has been known to contribute to anxiety, which will also deprive you of joy. Wheat stops serotonin from being generated, hence leading to depression. Alcohol is related to moodiness, and while some persons feel briefly happy after taking alcohol, the sensation often fades into pessimism.

Supplements to Consider

Vitamin C has been demonstrated to lower cortisol, which is the hormone that causes stress. Unless you are obtaining a large quantity of this vitamin through your food, a daily supplement is an excellent option.

Because a folic acid deficit has been related to depression, you may consider taking a supplement. Omega-3 fatty acids and vitamin B12 are also good for a natural mood boost. Supplements that can help you curb unhealthy appetites include vitamin B complex, Co-Enzyme Q10, and resveratrol.

Because food has such a large influence on your mood, you would be prudent to exploit it to its maximum capacity. Instead of merely picking your food based on what you want at the time, transform your plate into a potent weapon that will battle sadness and anxiety, and create and sustain your happiness.

You deserve the opportunity to experience pleasure, and by adjusting your eating habits you may transform your life for the better. Choose your mood by selecting your meal, and watch the difference it makes.

Chapter 5: Seven Phrases to Increase Your Happiness

There are numerous ways you may boost your happiness and many techniques that don't need much planning or effort.

Our words have power, and by repeating mantras to yourself throughout your day, you will discover that feeling joyful starts to come effortlessly to you. Here are seven mantras that, when repeated regularly, may improve your life.

I Am Amazing

These three phrases may help prevent you from sliding into a depression of self-hate. Too many folks do not have regard for themselves and forget that they are great, attractive and one of a kind. Repeat this phrase repeatedly so the words will come to you when you need them the most.

I Am Grateful

Gratefulness is a guaranteed approach to obtaining happiness. When you are thankful, you are making an effort to remind yourself of the positive things in your life. In turn, this cheerful mindset attracts even more excellent things.

I Love Myself at All Times

One of life's most crucial lessons is to love oneself. If you feel as if you haven't yet reached a position of complete self-love and respect, then repeat these phrases until you do. Say them when you are satisfied with yourself, as well as when you are furious and disappointed with yourself.

I Am a Magnet for Good Things

Believing that wonderful thing and pleasant experiences are going your way, can assist them to do so. Thinking of oneself as a magnet to everything great will bring those things to you. Your self-confidence and good attitude attract what they give out, and you will witness your life becoming enhanced as you repeat this phrase regularly.

I Attract Healthy People into My Life

Even under the finest conditions, the wrong individuals will hinder us from getting far. Create a group of people who are optimistic just like you are. Avoid drama, and repeat this phrase to yourself anytime you are tempted to be drawn into someone's bad energy.

I Can Do Anything I Set My Mind To

Believing in yourself and having faith in what you can do can lead you far. When you know that you can achieve everything you put your mind to, you will discover endless enjoyment in that knowledge. Speak these words when you are striving to alter your circumstances, and know that you have the power it takes to accomplish it.

I Have a Purpose

No matter how much money a person earns or how much they achieve, life will seem worthless and lifeless without a sense of purpose. There are many books produced on the topic that may help you assess your life and figure out what your special mission is.

Think about the things you enjoy and are attracted to, and what gives you your greatest sense of fulfillment. You have something unique to give the world, and this slogan reminds you of that reality.

Our words contain enormous power, and mantras are a terrific method to start us on the road to happiness. When you utilize your words to bring wonderful things into your life, you will discover happiness. Repeat these mantras and find out what a difference they will make for you.

Chapter 6: 11 Ways to Increase Your Happiness

For as much as we desire happiness, we may not be the greatest at evaluating whether or not we have enough of it... or what it is.

Though the notion of happiness may seem easy, it's really hard to nail down.

One of the first ways we get confused is by supposing happiness is a continual state of being. But happiness is an emotion the same way anger and sorrow are feelings. It's normal to experience more or less of a specific feeling at various seasons of your life.

In the era of social media when you may be comparing your day-to-day with someone else's highlight reel, it might be difficult to judge how much pleasure you typically feel and how much happiness is normal for you.

Overall happiness may be impacted by numerous things, according to a study from 2019. This might include:

- Overall optimism
- Enjoying activities
- A feeling of mission
- Financial
- Security
- Gratitude
- Positive connections

Happiness is also extremely customized. One individual may feel pleased while engaging with people while another may feel their best when spending time outside.

What seems to be true across the board is that having a clear grasp of what makes you happy makes it simpler to encourage happiness in your life.

11 Ways to Increase Your Happiness

Increasing happiness can seem like a large undertaking — yet occasionally, a little action can have a profoundly good influence on your mood.

It's not always simple to tell what would help you feel happy, particularly when you've been feeling low for a long.

Whether you're searching for a fast mood boost or are aiming to develop good habits, you can benefit from trying these science-backed techniques to raise your happiness.

Here are some suggestions:

1. Make sure your fundamental requirements are covered

Before we get into the enjoyable things, let's speak about your fundamental necessities.

Your mood is directly impacted by elements like sleep and diet. To give your brain the foundation it needs to be joyful, you need to be nourished and well-rested.

If your mood is poor, try asking yourself:

- Have I received enough sleep?
- Have I had a healthy meal recently?
- Did I drink enough water today?

Often, you could feel moody without recognizing that it's because you're sleepy or hungry. In such instances, improving happiness may be as easy as eating, taking a sleep, or drinking a glass of water.

2. Get Inventive

When did you last take time out of your day to accomplish something creative simply for fun?

You may use paint to express and process your feelings or as a joyful activity that just provides you pleasure. Creative hobbies may also help alleviate symptoms of depression.

Doing something creative may provide you with a feeling of success and increase your self-esteem.

You could discover that one of the following creative activities provides you with joy:

- Dancing
- Collaging
- Coloring or sketching
- Embroidery,
- Crocheting, or knitting
- Digital art
- Writing fiction, poetry, or music
- Baking or cooking
- Spotter
- Gardening

- Beading
- Playing an instrument

And if the ultimate result isn't a masterpiece, that's great. Your creative output doesn't have to be "excellent," simply good for you.

3. Start a gratitude practice

Taking time to dwell on joyful moments, positive things that occurred in your day, or individuals you admire in your life may be a pleasant mood boost.

Remembering positive memories might provide some useful perspective when you're feeling depressed, providing a reminder that good times exist and your negative mood won't endure forever.

One technique to promote thankfulness is to try writing down things you're grateful for frequently. This may take as little as 5 minutes a day.

Researchers in a 2019 clinical research of 1,337 participants discovered that completing a daily appreciation list for 14 days can promote positive emotions and boost feelings of contentment.

Similarly, researchers in a 2021 review concluded that “individuals who feel greater thankfulness had reduced levels of depression” and advised more studies should look at how gratitude may assist with depression.

Consider getting into the practice of writing down things you’re thankful for. You may also try speaking it out loud to yourself or a loved one.

4. Try Journaling

Journaling is a technique to increase your mood with a simple pen and paper. According to 2018 research, expressive writing might offer both mental and physical health advantages.

There are several mental health advantages of journaling. It may help you digest your emotions, communicate your sentiments, and think through a challenging issue. It may also enhance self-awareness and help you to figure out what your values are and what's important to you.

5. Spend some time in nature

Spending time in nature may improve emotions of contentment and lessen stress.

Researchers in a 2022 study trusted Source revealed that rates of sadness and anxiety were greater during the COVID-19 pandemic compared with pre-pandemic days. But persons who spent more time in green space had substantially lower anxiety and depression ratings than those who spent less time in nature.

Experts suggest spending at least 120 minutes on trusted Sources in nature each week. If that's not practicable for you, even a few minutes could assist.

Hiking outdoors is excellent, but if that's not your thing, consider the following:

Plan a day at the beach or a forest with loved ones.
Eat outdoors, whether at restaurants or home.
Have your morning coffee in your yard, balcony, or in a neighborhood park.
Visit a park for a 15-minute rest.
Walk your dog through a leafy area.
Go for a stroll while listening to guided walking meditation.

6. Get some sunlight

Sunlight is connected with a range of advantages, both mental and physical. It plays a function in regulating the circadian rhythm, which informs the body when to sleep and when to wake up. This influences our emotions.

Sunlight boosts the creation of vitamin D, which many of us are lacking in. Various research, including a 2018 review, describe how vitamin D insufficiency may have associations with depression.

7. Listen to music that makes you joyful

Listening to music may have stress-relieving benefits. Upbeat music, particularly music you identify with as a happy experience, could put a grin on your face.

Consider the following ideas:

- Search for pleasant, cherry playlists on YouTube, Spotify, or iTunes.
- Try listening to mainstream music from a few years ago. The nostalgia could raise your mood.
- Listen to the music from your favorite movies or games.
- Make a “happy playlist” for when you need a mood boost in the future.

8. Exercise

You probably have heard this before, but exercise can enhance your mental health.

Physical exercise may boost the release of feel-good chemicals including dopamine, serotonin, and endorphins. A 2017 experiment indicated that even a little exercise might help relieve the symptoms of depression.

If working exercise isn’t your thing, you may just make it your aim to move more. You might take your dog or a neighbor's dog for a walk, do some jumping jacks on your lunch break, or check out a yoga DVD.

It helps to choose a form of workout that makes you happy and motivated to keep it up. Some individuals find the following exercises entertaining and engaging:

- Dance
- Tennis
- Stream sports
- Rock climbing or bouldering
- Trampolining
- Frisbee
- Bike rides

9. Meditation

There's a reason why meditation has such a favorable reputation. Meditation and mindfulness could increase your mood, both in the long run and immediately.

During a 2021 study done in Hong Kong, researchers discovered that those who exercised mindfulness were "more likely to perceive happy life situations and feel appreciative for them." This includes experiencing delight while looking forward to things, recalling pleasant events, and making the most of good occasions.

Meditation could favorably impact the brain, boosting attention and lowering stress. If you've tried meditation and found it tough, you may find a different style of meditation to be more pleasurable.

10. Join a support group

Support groups, whether online or in person, maybe a terrific way to interact with individuals who have had similar experiences to you. Support groups may provide you comfort and help you help yourself.

You may discover local support groups using Google, on social media, or by contacting a local church, community center, or doctor's office.

11. Therapy

Talk therapy may help you develop your self-awareness, address potentially harmful patterns in your behavior and thinking, and process difficult events. In other words, it's a fantastic approach to invest in your mental health and boost your happiness in the long run.

You don't need to have a mental disease to go to therapy. Almost anybody can benefit from treatment.

If you find it difficult to feel joyful or content, or if you regularly find yourself feeling depressed, nervous, or overwhelmed, it can be an indication to chat with a therapist.

Chapter 7: Why Living in the Moment Makes You Happier

We all know that living in the past can weigh a person down, but why? And what about living in the future?

We need balance, yet living in the now is something we must concentrate on if we are to lead happy lives. Living in the now has been demonstrated to be the greatest method to become and remain happy. Here is why.

We Can't Change the Past

Almost every one of us has regrets over something in our past, but there is nothing we can do to alter it. Instead of squandering our time and energy in lament over things that are long gone and no longer in our ability to alter, we may utilize the energy to make our current condition better. Learn what you can from the past, and then move on.

We Can't Predict What the Future Holds

Don't worry about the future, since you cannot foretell what it may bring. You can only prepare to a certain amount, and being scared about what tomorrow brings will only generate tension that will lead to physical and mental issues.

Live in the now and choose to make the present your focus. Instead of dreading what effects your actions may bring to your future, make selections focused on what is beneficial in your life right now at this time. This will minimize inclinations towards despair and dread.

It Forces You to Be Present

When we focus more on the past or the future than the present, we slip away from what is there in front of our eyes. Maybe your present comprises a job endeavor that takes your whole focus and energy. Maybe your gift contains tiny children with runny noses who need lunch placed on the table.

When you accept your present completely, you will receive more out of the life you have. You will finally be able to stop destroying your current delight with anxiety about what may happen later, or the guilt of actions that are now in the past.

Be glad for the faces in front of you today, and for the chances that are knocking on your door at this precise now. The times you learn to treasure will improve your future with the nice memories you will take there, and you will have no regrets about misguided attention.

Having a Balanced Outlook

Living in the moment is crucial. Having a balanced concentration is vital too. When you think about the future, create the arrangements that are essential for you to appreciate that time later, since eventually, the future will be your "in the now." Don’t abandon your preparation for the future, but don’t allow it to overwhelm your life in an unhealthy manner. Balance is vital, and will enable you not to experience tension due to too much attention on one subject.

Living in the now is one of the finest things you can do for yourself. Happiness is gained when we choose to live and appreciate where we are right now, instead of pining away for another time and place. By using the time and the life you are given right now and now, you will feel genuine happiness.

Chapter 8: Hormones and Happiness

Hormones play a huge part in this sensation, and we are smart to understand the variables they play in this area and what we can do to maximize them.

How Hormones Work

Hormones are unique chemical messengers that govern most of the body's operations. The endocrine glands manufacture these particular signals and our body depends on them to operate correctly.

How we treat our bodies and the stuff we surround ourselves with makes a difference in how these hormones can benefit us. By studying what they do and how we may aid them in accomplishing their job, we will be closer to our objective of happiness.

What Hormones Are Related to Happiness?

Various hormones might improve one's happiness. The important ones contain serotonin, oxytocin, and dopamine.

Serotonin has been pretty widely recognized in recent decades. It is a neurotransmitter, which transfers signals from one section of the brain to another. Serotonin is vital in avoiding depression and other mental disorders, and issues develop when you have either a deficiency of this hormone or when it is unable to accomplish its work.

Oxytocin is regarded as the "love hormone" and has several responsibilities, which include helping individuals enhance their social skills and lowering fear.

Dopamine is another neurotransmitter, and it is triggered when a pleasant and unexpected scenario arises - which is why it is renowned for its function in helping the brain learn about rewards.

Natural Ways to Balance Your Hormones

Hormones need to maintain a tight balance to enable you to perform at optimal levels. Too much or too little of any hormone will produce short- and long-term concerns health-wise. Because our happiness is based on this, we are advised to try our best to achieve a healthy balance for all the hormones in our body, to create an atmosphere that encourages feeling good.

Some vital measures to maintain your hormones in excellent balance and operating order are to obtain adequate sleep each night, exercise frequently, and avoid pollutants from your everyday life. Minimize stress in your life as much as possible, and avoid birth control medications whenever feasible.

Foods to Balance Your Hormones

Food has a vital function in the balancing of hormones. There are numerous meals that you should make a point of consuming regularly, and several you should attempt to avoid.

Foods and nutrients that assist your body to regulate hormones and keep you happy include healthy fats such as those found in coconut oil, avocados, almonds, and wild salmon. Vitamin D is a crucial vitamin, as is magnesium. An adequate number of clean proteins should be consumed, as well as lots of veggies.

Your hormones play a crucial part in your sensations of happiness. Keeping them balanced and operating for you appropriately is crucial to guarantee emotions of mental well-being. By following the suggestions above, you will be able to regulate your hormones and live a life of pleasure and contentment.

Chapter 9: 8 Important Factors Underlying the Production of Happy Hormones

Research on actual happiness, carried out by Harvard University over 75 years, showed that the people we surround ourselves with, as well as our acceptance into society, may have a good influence on our physical and mental health and help us live longer.

Happiness chemicals that the body is capable of making by itself include dopamine, which makes us feel good; serotonin, which lessens sadness; and endorphins, which make us joyful and so assist to relieve physical pain.

How do we define individual happiness?

Factors contributing to happiness may range from person to person, and include:

- Doing the things you wish to do and having the flexibility to pick your route in life.
- Maintaining strong connections and being accepted within society.
- Feeling pleased with your circumstances and not comparing yourself negatively to others.
- Maintaining a cheerful attitude and not allowing oneself to get angry or put off by the various changes that occur throughout life.
- Achieving objectives that you have set out for yourself and staying optimistic whilst striving to attain them.
- Keeping healthy both mentally and physically, therefore lowering the chance of getting sickness and disease.

Research on what creates a happy life, given by Robert Waldinger from Harvard University, took over 75 years to complete and looked into the lives of 724 volunteers, as well as their spouses and other family members, bringing the total number of individuals investigated to over 2,000. After evaluating the data, a definite association was identified between strong relationships, excellent health, and happiness.

Maintaining strong connections was also proven to aid individuals halt the aging process and allow them to live longer lives.

8 Elements that Stimulate the Generation of Happy Hormones:

1. Exercise

Exercise not only keeps us fit and healthy but also protects us against sickness and degeneration. It boosts the synthesis of numerous hormones, including:

- Development hormones that are vital to repair and growth.

- Testosterone helps to rejuvenate and energize the body and stimulates muscular development.

- Insulin and thyroid hormones serve to control blood glucose levels and improve metabolism.

Additionally, exercise may aid the brain in creating hormones connected with pleasure, such as:

- Dopamine is the hormone responsible for making us feel happy. If we can attain our body shape or weight objectives, this hormone will be generated in bigger amounts.

- Serotonin, which may help lessen the symptoms of depression.

- Endorphins are directly associated with happiness, meaning they may aid to lessen physical pain or signs of damage in our muscles owing to their chemical features being comparable to morphine, which is utilized for pain treatment.

2. Partaking in Gratifying Activities that put a Grin on Your Face

Visiting new locations, having a soothing massage, or indulging in activities that put a smile on your face, whether they include family members, friends, or loved ones, may all give a welcome break from the tension and troubles that may collect in our everyday lives. Furthermore, having a grin on your face while experiencing challenging situations might boost the body's creation of serotonin and endorphins, both of which are directly related to pleasure.

3. Light Exposure to Sunshine

In addition to acquiring vitamin D from different fish, fish livers, and egg yolks, exposing the body to sunshine during the early morning or evening period (being sure to avoid the hours between 10:00 – 15:00) also assists the skin's generation of vitamin D. This vitamin not only helps to maintain our bones and immune system at full power but also indirectly encourages the creation of serotonin, a hormone capable of alleviating the symptoms linked with sadness.

4. Eating Chocolate (in Moderation)

Studies have revealed that ingesting roughly 50–100 grams of dark chocolate (equal to 300–600 calories) 1–2 times a week might lessen a person's odds of an early loss of life arising from heart disease when compared to those who do not consume any chocolate at all. Chocolate includes vital compounds which promote circulation and assist to strengthen coronary arteries. Dark chocolate , manufactured from 70–85% actual cocoa, is particularly beneficial in this respect.

Although dark chocolate contains limited levels of sugar and milk, it still should not be regarded as fully healthy and should thus only be taken in moderation.

5. Focus on Consuming Meals that are Rich in Tryptophan

Tryptophan is an important amino acid that the body is unable to manufacture by itself. Tryptophan may be derived from milk, butter, egg yolks, meat, fish, turkey, peanuts, almonds, dried dates, bananas, cottage cheese, and other high-protein foods. The body can employ this chemical to assist in the creation of serotonin and in the neurological processes that make us feel joyful. Moreover, tryptophan interacts with folic acid and iron to aid the body in forming red blood cells.

6. Playing with Pets

You may have noticed that your stress levels are decreased by playing with pets. This is because our connection with cats, dogs, or other pets that show us affection may raise the body's production of chemicals related to pleasure, including serotonin and oxytocin (a hormone connected to love and relationships) (a hormone linked to love and relationships).

7. Hugging or Kissing a Loved One

Hugs and kisses between people may be used to demonstrate affection, compassion, protection, and desire. We typically undertake these acts with someone we love which, in turn, leads to the body creating a variety of distinct hormones:

- Endorphins - the happy chemicals – are related to experiencing charmed.
-
- Dopamine is created when we feel fulfilled, resulting in feeling joyful, enthusiastic, and stimulated.
-
- Oxytocin is connected to relationships and allows us to develop links with other human beings.

8. Meditating

Meditation is a sort of spiritual comfort that may be good after a day full of emotional events that might leave us feeling low. Meditating, by taking in slowly and deeply before releasing that air just as gently, will help you gradually cleanse your thoughts of whatever negativity you may have gathered that day. Just being alone with your thoughts for a few seconds might allow you to achieve awareness and acceptance of some tough circumstances, leaving you with a more optimistic viewpoint. Meditating for at least 30 minutes has also been demonstrated to lower the production of cortisol, a hormone released during stressful situations, and replace it with endorphins which are responsible for feelings of relaxation.

Endorphins also provide a cheerful and refreshed sensation, reducing the aging process and increasing the body's immune system while simultaneously altering brain waves to guarantee a peaceful mind for a better night's sleep.

Conclusion

Although happiness implies various things to different individuals, our life experiences and other external elements such as social standing, education, professional popularity, health, responsibilities, and accomplishments all have a part to play in making our life full.

Some of these may combine to assist you to reach your objectives, while others may demand no little amount of devotion to allow you to succeed. Nevertheless, every individual is capable of creating success in their life in one way or another, which will provide them the greatest opportunity of feeling happy and pleased subsequently

www.ingramcontent.com/pod-product-compliance
Lightning Source LLC
LaVergne TN
LVHW052055160826
845678LV00015B/3242

* 9 7 9 8 3 6 2 9 6 0 1 9 3 *